WHAT'S IT LIKE TO LIVE HERE?
SMALL TOWN

BY KATIE MARSICO

Published in the United States of America by Cherry Lake Publishing
Ann Arbor, Michigan
www.cherrylakepublishing.com

Content Adviser: James Wolfinger, PhD, Associate Professor, Department of History,
DePaul University, Chicago, Illinois
Reading Adviser: Marla Conn, ReadAbility, Inc.

Photo Credits: Cover and page 1, ©Tetra Images/Alamy; page 5, ©XiXinXing/Shutterstock,
Inc.; page 7, ©Anne Kitzman/Shutterstock, Inc.; page 9, ©Hurst Photo/Shutterstock, Inc.;
page 11, ©Kzenon/Shutterstock, Inc.; page 13, ©bikeriderlondon/Shutterstock, Inc.; page 15,
©Lissandra Melo/Shutterstock, Inc.; page 17, ©Richard Thornton/Shutterstock, Inc.; page 19,
©Johnny Adolphson/Shutterstock, Inc.; page 21, ©XiXinXing/Shutterstock, Inc.

LIBRARY OF CONGRESS CATALOGING-IN-PUBLICATION DATA
Marsico, Katie, 1980– What's It Like to Live Here?:
  Small town / by Katie Marsico.
      pages cm. — (Community connections)
  Includes bibliographical references and index.
  ISBN 978-1-62431-567-1 (lib. bdg.) — ISBN 978-1-62431-591-6 (ebook) —
ISBN 978-1-62431-583-1 (pbk.) — ISBN 978-1-62431-575-6 (pdf)
  1. Small cities—Juvenile literature. I. Title.
  HT153.M374 2013
  307.76'2—dc23   2013026731

Cherry Lake Publishing would like to acknowledge the
work of The Partnership for 21st Century Skills. Please
visit www.p21.org for more information.

Printed in the United States of America
Corporate Graphics Inc.
January 2014

SMALL TOWN

CONTENTS

HI, NEIGHBOR!

Lizzy's dad pushed their shopping cart to the car. He always stopped to **greet** people he knew. This was nearly everyone in the parking lot. Most people know each other in Lizzy's small **community**. Lizzy smiled. She liked knowing the people around her. She felt lucky to be growing up in a small town!

Most people living in a small town often know each other.

Are small towns closer to major cities or the countryside? Make a guess. Actually, they are found in both locations! Yet most small towns are in rural areas. For example, take the town of Granum in Alberta, Canada. It sits on the border between a prairie and the Rocky Mountain foothills.

5

Small towns are not as large as cities. A town like Lizzy's has only a few hundred people. Other small towns have tens of thousands of people! Sometimes small towns **govern** themselves. For example, Lizzy's town had a mayor. Other towns have city councils. In other cases, officials at the city or state level govern them.

Small towns cover a far smaller geographic area than cities do.

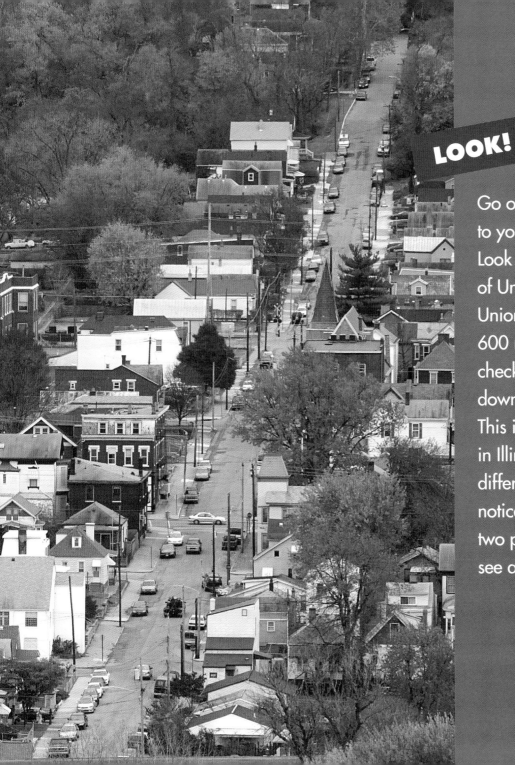

LOOK!

Go online or head to your local library. Look up pictures of Union, Illinois. Union has about 600 residents. Next, check out photos of downtown Chicago. This is a major city in Illinois. What differences do you notice between these two places? Can you see any similarities?

7

WORK AND PLAY

Lizzy's mom woke her in the morning. Lizzy dressed and ate breakfast before leaving for school. Her mother drove her there and back each day. Usually, Lizzy met her friend Kyle outside the school. He rode the bus to school.

Students might have a long bus ride if they attend school in another town.

Do you know people who grew up in small towns? Ask them how many people lived in their communities. How do the numbers they mention compare to one another?

Lizzy attended the only elementary school in her town. She knew almost all the kids in her grade. Most of them lived in the same town as Lizzy. Other students came from nearby towns.

Small towns have fewer schools than cities do.

THINK!

What kinds of pets do kids in small towns have? Many own the same kinds of animals as people in bigger communities. They have dogs, cats, fish, and birds. Some rural small-town residents may also keep farm animals. They might have horses, cows, chickens, or sheep.

After school, Lizzy finished her homework right away. Then she walked Pete, the family dog. She liked to wave to her neighbors as she walked.

On weekends, Lizzy spent time with friends. Sometimes she visited Kyle. They played basketball in his driveway.

Small-town kids have plenty of space to play games and climb trees.

Where do you think people in small towns work? There is no one answer. Some small-town residents work on farms. Many work in shops or offices within their community. Other residents **commute**. Commuters travel to nearby cities to work.

13

Small towns have less public **transportation** than cities do. People get from place to place using cars or bikes. Lizzy and her family sometimes liked to rely on their feet. The family's doctor was within walking distance. So was the park. Lizzy liked to walk there if the weather was nice.

People in small towns might live close enough to businesses to walk to work.

LOOK!

Find a map of a small town in your area. Then check out a map of a nearby major city. Does one community have more roads than the other? Does what you see surprise you?

15

TAKING PART

Small-town kids have a lot of opportunities to know their neighbors. Lizzy's town had everything from picnics to community festivals. Lizzy always looked forward to parades. One was held every summer. Marching bands played music. Local businesses and community leaders handed out candy. Residents showed up to talk and share snacks.

Local school marching bands are often seen in small-town parades.

Talk to friends and family who grew up in small towns. Ask how close they were to their neighbors. Also find out if they lived in a diverse community. Did residents share similar backgrounds? Or did they belong to different races and religions?

17

Lizzy's parents liked to attend town meetings. Residents discuss important community issues at these meetings. Once, Lizzy's dad suggested adding more stop signs in the town. He thought they would be useful at busy intersections. The mayor and other town residents discussed it and agreed.

Residents in Lizzy's town worked together to determine whether the town needed more stop signs.

Think about your community's government. Is there a mayor? Does anyone in your family ever attend community meetings? Name some ways you work with neighbors and local officials.

A CLOSE COMMUNITY

Lizzy liked having friendships with her neighbors. She also admired her parents. She wanted to take part in improving her community, too. Lizzy asked her parents to take her to a town meeting. She loved her small town. She wanted to be part of what shaped it in the future!

Small towns are the perfect place to learn the rewards of friendship and teamwork.

Fold a large piece of paper in half. Draw a picture of a small town on the left side. Sketch a big city on the right side. Show examples of a few people living in each community. How are they getting from place to place? How well do they know one another?

GLOSSARY

community (kuh-MYOO-nut-ee) a place and the people who live there

commute (kuh-MYOOT) to travel some distance to work or school each day, usually by car, bus, or train

diverse (dye-VURS) having many different types or kinds

govern (GUHV-urn) to control or exercise authority over a country, organization, or group

greet (GREET) to give a sign of welcome when you meet someone

rural (ROOR-uhl) having to do with the countryside or farming

transportation (trans-pur-TAY-shuhn) a way of moving people from one place to another

FIND OUT MORE

BOOKS

Bodden, Valerie. *A Town*. Mankato, MN: Creative Education, 2008.

McDonald, Caryl. *Rural Life, Urban Life*. New York: Rosen Publishing, 2013.

Pancella, Peggy. *Small Town*. Chicago: Heinemann Library, 2006.

WEB SITES

BrainPOP Jr.—Rural, Suburban, and Urban
www.brainpopjr.com/socialstudies/communities /ruralsuburbanandurban/preview.weml
Learn more about life in different community settings, including suburbs, rural areas, and cities.

Houghton Mifflin Company—Types of Communities
www.eduplace.com/kids/socsci/books/applications/imaps/maps /g3_u1/
Use this interactive map to complete a variety of online activities connected to suburban, urban, and rural communities.

INDEX

ABOUT THE AUTHOR

Katie Marsico is the author of more than 100 children's books. She lives in a suburb of Chicago, Illinois, with her husband and children.